"What Am I?"

A Collection Of
Traditional Word Puzzles

VOLUME ONE

Zack Guido

ISBN-13: 978-1502896667
ISBN-10: 1502896664

*Dedicated to the open-minded, the gifted,
and the forward-moving.*

TABLE OF CONTENTS

INTRODUCTION

This is the first volume of a collection of traditional "What am I?" style word riddles. They typically rhyme and feel like limericks. The purpose of this book is to be both entertaining and mentally stimulating. Mixing an endearing child-like form of written word with an intellectual challenge helps to accentuate different ways of thinking while allowing for fun problem-solving.

The riddles all share some simple rules:

♦ They have one intended answer. Some may seem to have multiple solutions, but there was one specific solution in mind when they were written.

♦ Each line of each riddle is important and the answers fulfill all given clues.

♦ Some of the clues and solutions refer to homonyms or homophones, intended to add fun wordplay and an additional level of challenge. Always consider this as you are reading through them.

The book begins with a section with famous riddles from literature. Following that is a section with old classics that many riddle-lovers will already be familiar with. Finally, you will come across the main content of the book: seventy-five original yet traditional word riddles.

The solutions will be located on the next page, directly behind each riddle. They are intentionally hard to read, as to help avoid any accidental spoiling of answers you didn't want to see yet. Don't look unless you absolutely have to!

Enjoy.

FAMOUS RIDDLES

The Riddle Of The Sphinx

If the cover of this book felt relevant then you are probably familiar with the story of Oedipus, the Greek hero. When Oedipus travels to Thebes a sphinx that guards the entrance to the city greets him. The sphinx asks all visitors a riddle that they must answer correctly in order to be granted permission to enter. If the visitor guesses incorrectly, the sphinx will kill and eat them.

What walks on four feet in the morning,
Two in the afternoon,
And three at night?

Man.
(crawls as a child, walks as an adult, walks with a cane as an elder)

"The Hobbit" by J.R.R. Tolkien

In "The Hobbit" there are eight classically famous (and extremely difficult / borderline unfair) riddles. These are provided without context as to not spoil anything from the story:

An eye in a blue face,
Saw an eye in a green face.
"That eye is like to this eye,"
Said the first eye,
"But in low place, not in high place."
What am I?

Alive without breath,
As cold as death;
Never thirsty, ever drinking,
All in mail never clinking.
What am I?

Voiceless it cries,
Wingless flutters,
Toothless bites,
Mouthless mutters.
What am I?

"Sun on the daisies."
(Yes this is very difficult! Many would correctly argue too difficult.)

Fish

Wind

A box without hinges, key, or lid,
Yet golden treasure inside is hid.
What am I?

Thirty white horses on a red hill,
First they champ,
Then they stamp,
Then they stand still.
What am I?

This thing all things devours;
Birds, beasts, trees, flowers;
Gnaws iron, bites steel;
Grinds hard stones to meal;
Slays king, ruins town,
And beats high mountain down.
What am I?

Egg

Teeth

Time

No-legs lay on one leg,
Two-legs sat near on three legs,
Four-legs got some.
What am I?

It cannot be seen, cannot be felt,
Cannot be heard, cannot be smelt.
It lies behind stars and under hills,
And empty holes it fills.
It comes first and follows after,
Ends life, kills laughter.
What am I?

A fish on a table being eaten by a man on a stool and
a cat eating the bones of the fish.
(Yeah yeah yeah, I know. It's borderline impossible.)

Darkness

Harry Potter Meets A Sphinx

In "Harry Potter and the Goblet of Fire", the fourth installment of the Harry Potter series by J.K. Rowling, Harry crosses paths with a sphinx in a maze. The sphinx challenges him to a riddle, as a nod to the Oedipus story:

First think of the person who lives in disguise,
Who deals in secrets and tells naught but lies.
Next tell me what's always the last thing to mend,
The middle of middle and end of the end.
And finally give me the sound often heard,
During the search for a hard-to-find word.
Now string them together, and answer me this,
Which creature would you be unwilling to kiss?

Spider
("Spy" + "D" + "er")

Alice In Wonderland - The Unsolvable Riddle

"Alice's Adventures in Wonderland", the classic 1865 novel by Lewis Carroll (known by his mother as Charles Lutwidge Dodgson), is full of truly insane wordplay. It is a fantasy tale about a girl who travels to a world of complete nonsense.

During a tea party with a character known as The Mad Hatter, Alice is asked this riddle:

Why is a raven like a writing desk?

"I haven't the slightest idea."

That is the answer given to Alice by The Mad Hatter when she asks him for the solution.

Lewis Carroll's intention was that this riddle have no real answer, though after receiving many letters from readers who were curious about the riddle he provided some possible answers in the preface of a future edition of the book:

> "Enquiries have been so often addressed to me, as to whether any answer to the Hatter's Riddle can be imagines, that I may as well put on the record here what seems to me to be a fairly appropriate answer: 'Because it can produce a few notes, though they are very flat; and it is nevar put with the wrong end in front!' This however, is merely an afterthought; the riddle as originally invented had no answer at all."

Notice the wordplay with the intentional misspelling of "never" as "nevar", which is "raven" being spelled with its wrong end in front (backwards). Never a dull moment with Lewis Carroll.

CLASSIC RIDDLES

The following riddles are very much in the style of what you will find in the rest of the book. They are classics that many puzzle-lovers will be already familiar with.

In a way, this is prerequisite reading material for anyone who enjoys traditional "What Am I?" riddles:

The more I dry, the wetter I get.
What am I?

The more you take away from me, the bigger I get;
The more of me you put in something, the lighter it gets.
What am I?

Forwards I am heavy, backwards I am not.
What am I?

Towel

Hole

Ton

I leave every time you say my name.
What am I?

I'm lighter than a feather, but even the strongest man can only
hold me for a short time.
What am I?

I stay in a corner, but I travel around the world.
What am I?

Silence

Breath

Stamp

The poor have me;
The rich need me;
And you will die if you eat me.
What am I?

You can crack me;
You can make me;
You can tell me;
You can play me.
What am I?

Nothing

Joke

ORIGINAL RIDDLES

One way I'm loose, one way I'm tight;
Out with left, in with right.
What am I?

My full power comes when my makers are dead;
I await a heavy hat to put on my head.
What am I?

The more of me you take,
The more of me there are.
What am I?

Screw / Screwdriver

Prince

Footsteps

Three holes to hold me;
Some strength to throw me;
To do well at my job, you need to control me;
You throw me away, I always come back;
I come in many colors, but traditionally I'm black.
What am I?

I grow in the dark and shine in the light;
The paler I am, the more I am liked;
My maker never gets paid, but never goes on strike.
What am I?

Thursday before Tuesday;
Three before two;
Today before yesterday;
Me before you.
What am I?

Bowling Ball

Pearl

Dictionary

I have two bodies, joined as one;
Watch this trick: I'll flip, stand still, and run.
What am I?

I can be caught but I can't be thrown;
I'm harder to catch if you're always alone.
What am I?

On my feet I am a shield;
On my head I am a cup;
I can go up a chimney down,
But not down a chimney up.
What am I?

Hourglass

A Cold

Umbrella

A sentry in the dark;
I firmly stand my ground;
The longer I stand up,
The shorter I sit down.
What am I?

Always running, never walking;
Making noise but never talking;
I move what moves me;
Constantly thirsty.
What am I?

I can take you to the nines, and to thirteen too;
I can love, shine, beat, dig,
And do with or into shoes.
What am I?

Candle

Engine

Suit

I help to make you comfortable,
I must work while you're awake;
But when you're asleep I do my job,
And don't take a single break;
I'm partly a guard, I'm partly a case;
I'm not hard to move but I'm always in the exact same place.
What am I?

You always have me with you,
You always leave me behind;
But if you go and break the rules,
Then with some tools, someone else may try to find.
What am I?

I'm the beginning of every instant;
I'm the end of a quick hello;
When I'm alone, I stand tall on my own;
I come in at nine, and at fifty-three too;
You need me, you bleed me, so what is I really?
What am I?

Eyelid

Fingerprints

Iodine

I come in an unreal can;
Misspell my name and I'll blow a flame;
I taste good when faked, I dangle in lakes;
And with a book I become a man.
What am I?

I start out surrounded by rock;
They find me, they free me, and then they between me,
Between wood with some rubber on top.
What am I?

Brothers and sisters I have seven,
But really I used to have eight;
I'm the biggest and they stare from way over there,
But they're shocked when they find out my weight.
What am I?

Worm

Lead / Graphite

Jupiter

Right-side-up I am who I am,
Upside-down sometimes I stay the same;
I move up and down slightly,
And I'm scissor-ed quite nicely,
Plus I'm short for a twice-as-long name.
What am I?

I'm easy to look at but impossible to see;
An eight's an eight,
A three's an E,
And an E's a three to me.
What am I?

I can be a coat, but only when I'm wet;
People sometimes would like to watch me do what I do,
Rather than doing what you suggest.
What am I?

BOB

Mirror

Paint

I'm contained in a tube;
Warmer or cooler I move;
But don't try to freeze me,
It sure won't be easy.
What am I?

You can call me but I don't have a phone;
I might be in your apartment, probably not in your home;
I go through the ceiling; I go through the floor;
I don't have a handle, but I do have a door.
What am I?

I might cause some pleading,
I might cause some bleeding;
Hit me with a hammer,
And out I come speeding.
What am I?

Mercury

Elevator

Bullet

Zero has none,
The same as one;
Two has three,
The same as four;
But two have more.
What am I?

When first comes in second,
And second comes in first,
And first and second did the best,
But also did the worst.
What am I?

I'm made out of five letters,
And I'm made out of seven letters;
I have keys but I don't have locks,
I'm concerned with time, but not with clocks.
What am I?

Numbers On A Phone

Tie

Music / Piano

We come as five,
Sometimes six;
Rarely ever do we all hang together,
But with the rest of our friends,
We make a nice mix.
What am I?

I don't need shoes,
I don't have feet;
I can't cook a think,
But need heat to find something to eat.
What am I?

People love it when they see me,
I appear strictly and routinely;
I typically stay in the sky,
But can't float, move, or fly.
What am I?

Vowels

Snake

Rainbow

I will tell you what you want to know,
But only under pressure;
You stand up tall to ask me your question,
But can rarely stand my answer.
What am I?

You can hook me but I'm not a fish;
You can drive me but I have no wheels;
You can slice me but I stay in one piece.
What am I?

I only fall when big enough,
And only rise when small;
You feel me when I'm falling down,
But on the way back up you feel hardly at all.
What am I?

Scale

Golf Ball

Raindrop / Water

I roam the earth with four legs,
And with a tiny tail;
My home can also be on a spoon,
And even in your hair.
What am I?

You can find me in a pond,
But I cannot get wet;
If you're a blonde then I'm a blonde,
And if you're not I'm probably a brunette.
What am I?

When I'm standing first in line,
I matter not at all;
But switch my place and you will find,
That line is not as small.
What am I?

Moose / Mousse

Reflection

Zero

One of us can cause a riot,
Two can keep the peace;
We're similar in many ways,
But each is still unique;
One can show you truly care,
One can show you truly swear,
One can tell you bad or good;
You can't misplace us though we can be lost,
But it's okay, you'll have a spare.
What am I?

You have to give me to someone in order to keep me.
What am I?

People don't want me,
But once they get involved with me,
They don't want to lose me.
What am I?

Fingers

Your Word

Lawsuit

Some people point me,
Noble people take me,
Some people pass me,
And I'm a game some insist on playing.
What am I?

I can be drawn and still be nothing,
I can be shot and still be nothing;
The best way to take me away,
Is to fill me in with something.
What am I?

We're five little girls and we all look alike,
But we're equally different in our widths and our heights;
We live with each other but each have our own space,
But we can all stand together, in the exact same place;
We're usually happy, and we can't change the look on our face.
What am I?

Blame

Blank

Russian Dolls

Take your stick and hit me,
But you can't hit my friends,
That's my job and mine alone,
Don't scratch me at the end.
What am I?

Thirty men and just two ladies,
Having good old-fashioned fun;
Some matter more, and some matter less,
But any one can get the job done.
What am I?

One comes before the other,
The other comes before the one;
Like the chicken and the egg,
No one knows which one begun.
What am I?

Cue Ball

Chess Pieces

Day and Night

At night I'm told what to do,
At morning I do what I'm told;
The closer I come to doing my job,
The more you're getting old.
What am I?

I stand straight up, I'm hard to move,
I'm buried in the ground, I'm etched and grooved;
Once I'm yours, I'm yours to keep,
When people need me, others weep.
What am I?

I stand there blushing beside the road,
I give advice, do what you're told;
Legally speaking,
Please do it completely.
What am I?

Alarm Clock

Gravestone

Stop Sign

I stay right in place, guarding a space;
Many people hate me and get right in my face;
But they tend to stay for an hour or two,
You better pay me or I'll tell on you.
What am I?

To use me you dip me,
Some leave me, some jig me;
I work from a bag, unless you get fancy;
Use me too much and you might get antsy.
What am I?

I talk a lot at work, but never say what's on my mind;
I listen too, to wait for my cue;
And tend to say and hear the same thing many times.
What am I?

Parking Meter

Tea Bag

Actor

I don't have a color, but I can be white;
I'm not a magician, just a type of sleight;
I can cause much pain, and I can relieve;
I do my job best when people believe.
What am I?

I can be breaking, but cannot be broken;
I'm after-the-fact, I'm written and spoken;
I can be good, I can be bad too;
And in a certain way, I can have a yellowish hue.
What am I?

I have many keys, but only some are used for locking;
My partner does the moving, I do the talking.
What am I?

Lie

News

Computer Keyboard

You, just you, can walk with me,
But I will have to run;
Where we are when we begin,
Is where we are when we are done.
What am I?

People tend to lose me,
When things do not go right;
No one sees me until I'm lost,
I'm known to inspire fright.
What am I?

I come by the dozen,
And by thirty, too;
Sometimes even thirty-one,
But never thirty-two.
What am I?

Treadmill

Temper

Month

I'm known to be quick, but not known to be noticed;
I happen less often the more that you focus;
When I happen I'm two things at once,
And I happen thousands of times per day,
Every day, every month.
What am I?

I have hands that wave, but they can't wave goodbye;
I act like a clock, but I don't tell the time;
I hang, I stand, I swivel, I sit;
I can act like your mouth, but I can't swallow or spit.
What am I?

If I'm long I may be heavy,
I'm one thing that's made of many;
I'm a whole that's made of holes;
Sometimes I keep two things together,
Sometimes I just sit and pose.
What am I?

Blink

Electric Fan

Chain

Nobody wants to eat me, but they all end up taking a bite;
It's not that I am tempting, I'm a fate that they can't fight;
I sit on your shelf, but I'm not a book;
I'm in your kitchen cabinets, but you don't use me to cook;
I'm in your bedroom too, and your closet, and your den;
Week after week you get rid of me,
But I always come back again.
What am I?

I'm put on a horse, but not on it back;
And not on its feet, I don't leave a track;
Not in its hair, not on its face, I'm not put for style;
And I don't last long, just for a little while.
What am I?

I'm a type of language, but I'm not meant for speaking;
I'm found everywhere, but rarely do people read me;
I'm easy to write, and easy to understand,
But to translate a book into me would take years,
If you do it by hand.
What am I?

Dust

Bet / Wager

Binary

The lowest number's rank,
The highest rank of any;
I'm famously known as a crown that sank,
I'm sought after by many.
What am I?

I can't stand up unless I'm moving,
And I move fast but I don't move much;
When I move it's physics I'm proving,
Don't interrupt my motion, please, don't touch.
What am I?

Sometimes bought, sometimes sold,
Sometimes kept, sometimes told;
I'm most potent when I'm unexpected,
I make careers out of being intercepted.
What am I?

Gold

Spinning Top

Secret

I'm something very common, you see me all around;
I live on the water, in the air, on the ground;
But there's something not so common about me,
As I grow up, I grow down.
What am I?

When you're drunk you drive me wild,
And I always find you controlling;
You never bothered me when you were a child,
Just relax, I'll do all the rolling.
What am I?

I can hold a mountain up,
And keep down the whole sea;
The close you get, the further I stay,
You can run, run, run, but you can't catch up to me.
What am I?

Bird / Goose / Duck

Automobile

Horizon

Stiff little people on a field, standing in a row;
Though we're stiff we're nimble and swift,
We kick, we slide, we move side to side,
And round and round we go.
What am I?

When you sit down you have me,
When you stand I'm gone;
Sit again, I come right back,
Because I've been there all along.
What am I?

A taxicab for one,
I start when you are done;
I take you to your destination, then I go away,
If by chance you need a ride back,
Someone's made a grave mistake.
What am I?

Foosball Table

Lap

Hearse

I'm always on my way, steadily getting closer;
But just when I'm about to arrive,
I have to start all over.
What am I?

I come in different lengths, different sizes, similar shapes;
I need to be maintained, I can be painted, I can be fakes;
I typically come as twenty, typically five at a time.
What am I?

Every year on my birthday, I get a new ring;
But I never have room for another,
That is, until I get the freaking thing.
What am I?

Tomorrow

Nails

Tree

"AS HUMAN
BEINGS, WE
HAVE A NATURAL
COMPULSION TO
FILL EMPTY
SPACES."

-Will Shortz

58158635R00050

Made in the USA
Lexington, KY
03 December 2016